Unbelievable Pictures and Facts About Boxers

By: Olivia Greenwood

Introduction

A breed which can be a good protection dog, a police dog, a dog who is exceptionally good with children, and even a guide dog for a blind person, the Boxer is a great dog to have on your side!

What is the lifespan of Boxers?

The Boxer lives up to between 10-12 years old.

What kind of breed is a Boxer?

The watchful and alert Boxer is considered part of the Working Group category which means it is able to do important jobs such as rescuing people from water, pulling a sled, or guarding property.

Where is the Boxer from originally?

The Boxer is from Germany. It was one of the first breeds in Germany selected for police training.

How did the Boxer get its name?

The Boxer is an English name, referring to the way the dog will use its front paws in play or while defending itself - like a human boxer in the sport of boxing. The breed usually can stand on its back legs and "punch" its front paws - that's why it was named "boxer!"

How long has the Boxer existed?

The Boxer's ancestors may go back as far as 2500 BC, but the modern breed of Boxers came from the late 1800s.

Are Boxers noisy?

Boxers may bark to protect its territory, yet are not considered excessive barkers. If the Boxer is barking, there's a good reason. The bark of an adult Boxer is very deep.

What color can a Boxer not be?

Boxers are never solid black in color, although they can be solid white. One in four Boxers are all white.

What records have Boxers set?

A Boxer named Brandy set the record for having the longest tongue on a dog - measuring 17 inches!

What is the reason Boxers' noses are short?

They were bred this way to help clutch small animals in their mouths back in the time when they used for hunting.

Are Boxers a specific color?

A boxer is usually fawn, ranging from light tan to mahogany with brindle, which is a pattern that includes black stripes. Some Boxers have partial white markings, usually on their chests and paws. Their coats are shiny, smooth and very short haired.

Are these dogs associated with any war stories?

The Boxer's ancestors were used as war dogs. Continuing the job to the time of World War I, Boxers assisted German soldiers by carrying supplies and messages, and helping to find wounded soldiers on the battlefield.

Is the Boxer a good outdoor dog?

For exercising and running around, of course; yet boxers are not meant for outdoor living since they are sensitive to weather extremes.

How much exercise is good for a Boxer?

Since Boxers are busy, high-energy and strong dogs who like mental and physical challenges, they need plenty of exercise, however, they should not be allowed to run loose.

What year was the breed officially recognized?

The Boxer was recognized as a breed in 1904.

What words describe Boxers the best?

Some words which describe the typical Boxer are: fun-loving, playful, active, courageous, strong, bright, loyal, smart, good-looking, affectionate, and sometimes silly!

How popular is this breed in America?

The Boxer ranks 10 in popularity out of 193 breeds listed with the American Kennel Club. It is one of the most popular dog breeds in America and has been for a very long time.

What celebrities have or have owned Boxers?

It's reported that many celebrities love Boxers! Some actors and singers who own them (or have owned them) include Cameron Diaz, Luke Perry, Justin Timberlake, Hugh Jackman, Jennifer Love Hewitt, and race car driver Greg Biffle.

In what movies have Boxers appeared?

Not many Boxers have appeared in movies. One of the sled dogs in the movie, Chilly Dogs/Kevin of the North is a white boxer. Another Boxer is in the movie, Good Boy!

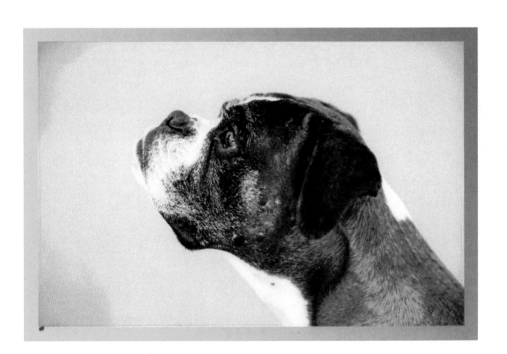

What is there to know about how to keep a Boxer clean?

A Boxer can collect "eye gunk" quickly; so its eye area should be kept clean. Also what needs to be kept clean is between the rolls in their faces, so as to prevent infection.

For how long is a Boxer considered a puppy?

Upon reaching 2 years old, the Boxer is considered an adult dog, however, they are slow to grow out of "puppyhood" and often do not mature until 3 years old.

Made in the USA
Middletown, DE
15 December 2019